DEADLY SCIENCE

Wild weather

Contents

ADJUNCT ASSOCIATE PROFESSOR COREY TUTT OAM

DEADLYSCIENCE

DeadlyScience aims to provide Science, Technology, Engineering and Mathematics (STEM) resources to remote schools around Australia. So far, DeadlyScience has shipped more than shipped more than 33,000 STEM books and resources to more than 800 schools across the country.

The organisation began when proud Kamilaroi man Corey Tutt found out that some schools in Australia were completely under-resourced and that Aboriginal and Torres Strait Islander children were discouraged from pursuing STEM because of this. DeadlyScience knows from personal experience that books and resources change lives and believes these kids deserve nothing but the best. Aboriginal and Torres Strait Islander peoples in Australia were the First Scientists of this land, and DeadlyScience is committed to preserving that history.

Australian seasons

For tens of thousands of years, First Nations Australians have used the behaviour of animals and changes in vegetation to identify different seasons. The Gadgerong people of the north-western Northern Territory have a three-season model, for example, while other groups have five or even six seasons.

First Nations groups from different areas use different types of markers to predict the change in seasons. The Gadgerong people, for instance, know that they are approaching the late dry season when march flies appear. This is a signal that crocodile eggs can be found and that it is time to search for native honey.

When settlers arrived in Australia, they brought with them a very European understanding of weather, including a four-season model (spring, summer, autumn and winter). Australia's weather patterns are very different, with some areas experiencing high rainfall for several months of the year, followed by long dry periods.

The seasons recognised by First Nations communities do a much better job of reflecting our climate than the European model. These diagrams show the seasons as understood by the Noongar people, the Dharawal people, and the Bininj/Mungguy peoples. The grey circle shows the months and the outer circle, coloured to reflect the temperature, shows the Indigenous name for the season. Around the outside, we've included samples of the markers that the groups use to identify the seasons.

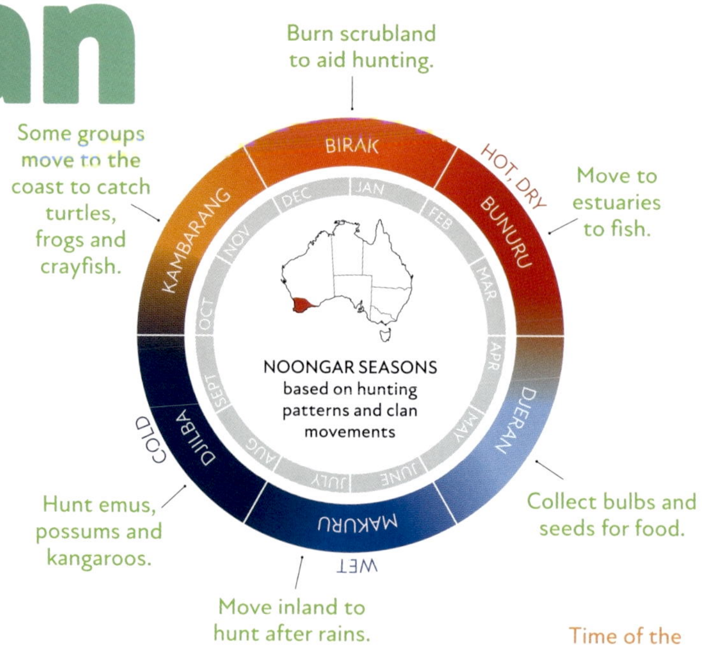

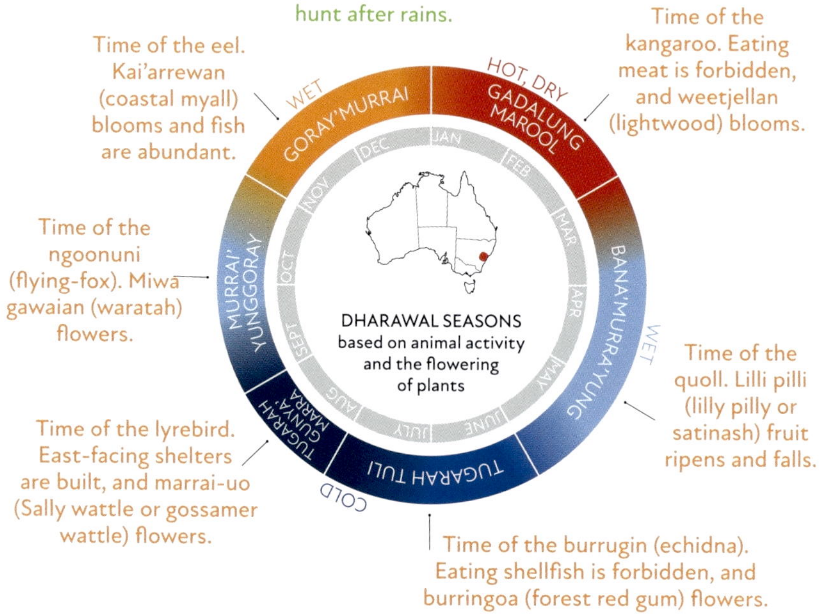

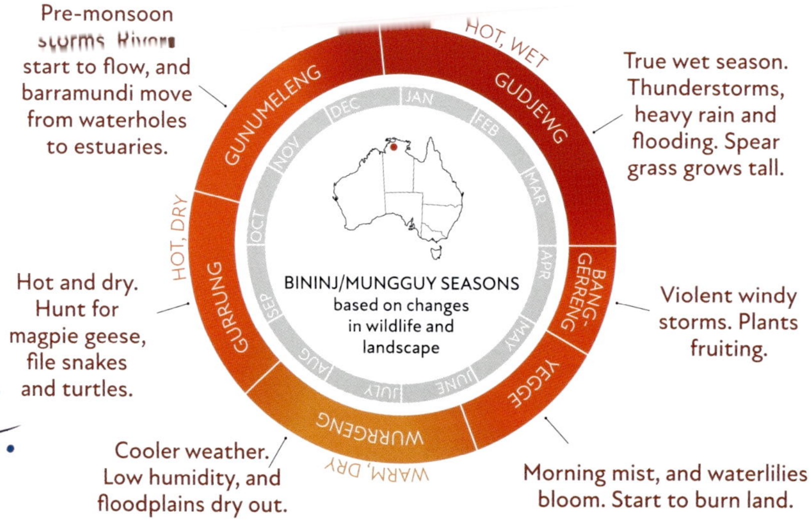

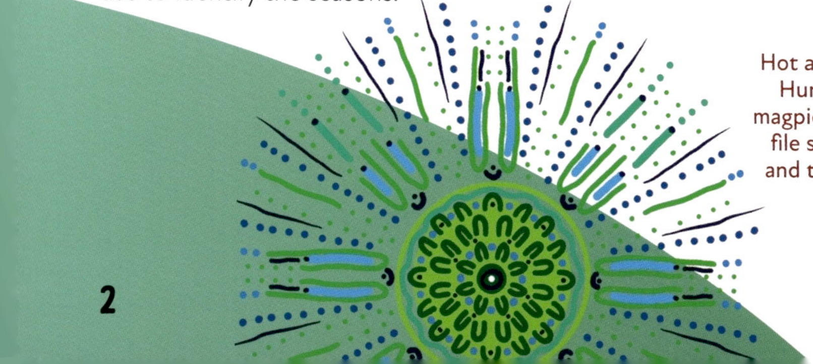

NOONGAR SEASONS based on hunting patterns and clan movements

- BIRAK (DEC–JAN) — Burn scrubland to aid hunting.
- BUNURU (FEB–MAR), HOT, DRY — Move to estuaries to fish.
- DJERAN (APR–MAY) — Collect bulbs and seeds for food.
- MAKURU (JUNE–JULY), WET — Move inland to hunt after rains.
- DJILBA (AUG–SEPT), COLD — Hunt emus, possums and kangaroos.
- KAMBARANG (OCT–NOV) — Some groups move to the coast to catch turtles, frogs and crayfish.

DHARAWAL SEASONS based on animal activity and the flowering of plants

- GADALUNG MAROOL (JAN–FEB), HOT, DRY — Time of the kangaroo. Eating meat is forbidden, and weetjellan (lightwood) blooms.
- BANA'MURRA'YUNG (MAR–MAY), WET — Time of the quoll. Lilli pilli (lilly pilly or satinash) fruit ripens and falls.
- TUGARAH TULI (JUNE–JULY), COLD — Time of the burrugin (echidna). Eating shellfish is forbidden, and burringoa (forest red gum) flowers.
- TUGARAH GUNYA'MARRA (AUG) — Time of the lyrebird. East-facing shelters are built, and marrai-uo (Sally wattle or gossamer wattle) flowers.
- MURRAI' YUNGGORAY (SEPT–OCT) — Time of the ngoonuni (flying-fox). Miwa gawaian (waratah) flowers.
- GORAY'MURRAI (NOV–DEC), WET — Time of the eel. Kai'arrewan (coastal myall) blooms and fish are abundant.

BININJ/MUNGGUY SEASONS based on changes in wildlife and landscape

- GUDJEWG (JAN–MAR), HOT, WET — True wet season. Thunderstorms, heavy rain and flooding. Spear grass grows tall.
- BANG-GERRENG (APR) — Violent windy storms. Plants fruiting.
- YEGGE (MAY–JUNE) — Morning mist, and waterlilies bloom. Start to burn land.
- WURRGENG (JUNE–AUG), WARM, DRY — Cooler weather. Low humidity, and floodplains dry out.
- GURRUNG (AUG–OCT), HOT, DRY — Hot and dry. Hunt for magpie geese, file snakes and turtles.
- GUNUMELENG (OCT–DEC) — Pre-monsoon storms. Rivers start to flow, and barramundi move from waterholes to estuaries.

Weather patterns

From droughts and bushfires to flooding rains and cyclones, Australia's climate is one of extremes. These cycles are heavily influenced by El Niño and La Niña, two opposite weather patterns that occur at almost the same time on opposite sides of the world. Climate change has the potential to make these cycles even more severe, which is worrying when we consider how damaging floods and bushfires can already be in Australia. Under normal conditions, trade winds blow from east to west across the Pacific, and warm waters blow across, bringing rain to the tropical areas of Australia and Asia.

WET SEASON STORM ON LARRAKIA COUNTRY IN DARWIN, NT

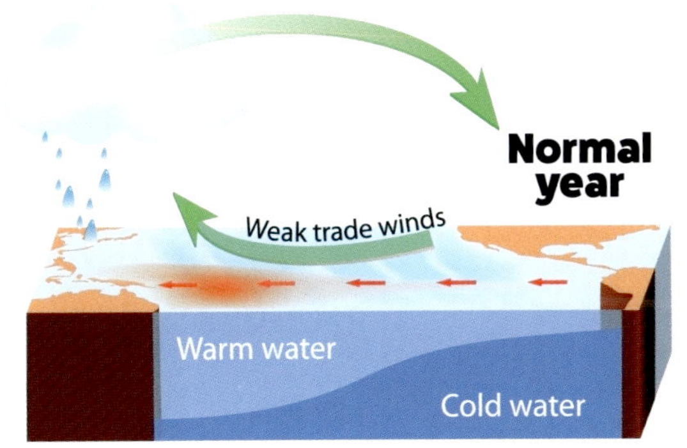

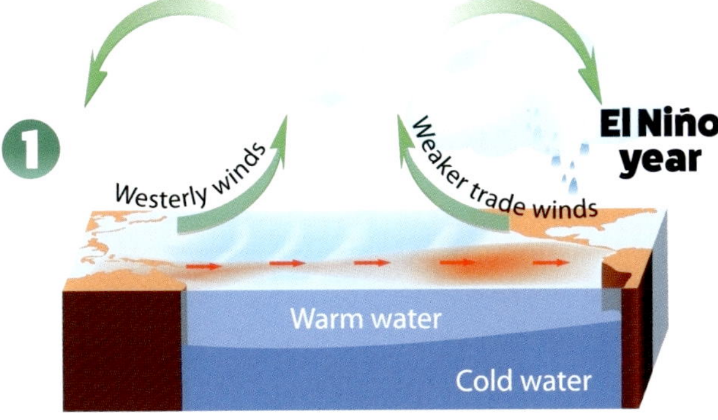

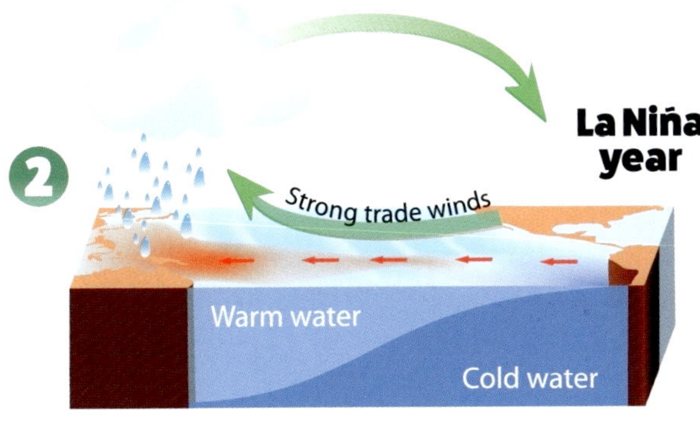

1 El Niño

El Niño occurs when the surface ocean waters in the eastern Pacific Ocean become abnormally warm and start to flow east, away from Australia and into the central Pacific Ocean. This flow of water is accompanied by air currents, which take with it rain-bearing clouds. This results in drier months in Australia and often droughts and bushfires. El Niño events occur every 4–7 years and usually last 12–18 months, peaking between December and April. The El Niño period during 2015–16 contributed to an early start to the bushfire season, as well as coral bleaching on the Great Barrier Reef.

While an El Niño event impacts the whole world, resulting in a hotter average temperature for the entire planet (by about 0.1 or 0.2 °C), its main effect is on countries in the Pacific, especially Australia, Indonesia, South America, and the smaller Pacific Island nations.

2 La Niña

La Niña is essentially the reverse weather pattern of El Niño. When there are El Niño events in Australia that cause droughts, there are likely to be La Niña events that cause floods in countries bordering the central and eastern tropical Pacific Ocean, including the west coast of the United States.

La Niña involves warm water, winds and rain-bearing clouds returning to our shores, often bringing with it flooding rains. In 2019–20, we experienced a La Niña pattern that brought the wettest summer in four years and the coolest daytime temperatures in more than nine years.

Fires

Bushfires are part of the Australian landscape. They have been around for an estimated 60 million years and are a regular cycle in our climate. The most devastating fires are usually preceded by record high temperatures, low relative humidity and strong winds, which create ideal conditions for the rapid spread of fire.

A COOL BURN IN THE APY LANDS, SA

Fire frequency

Australia is the driest inhabited continent, and many areas are covered in eucalypt forests that burn easily. Especially in summer, bushfires can spread quickly. There are fires every year and these can sometimes escalate to become a serious danger. South-eastern Australia often experiences particularly severe bushfires. Although these bushfires can claim lives, destroy homes and damage the environment, many native plants have developed characteristics that actually promote the spread of fire, since it can be necessary for the regeneration of the land and its plants.

Fire control

For thousands of years, First Nations people used a form of land management that involved 'cool' burns. These smaller, controlled fires meant bushfires were often smaller and less intense. Caring for Country in this way is important, and many of these principles are now being used in areas around Australia to prevent the occurrence of bigger and more destructive fires.

Firestorms

Bushfires may be ignited by lightning from thunderstorms that produce little or no rain. When flames become so intense that they create and sustain their own wind system, a firestorm forms. Firestorms can spread rapidly up slopes when strong winds are channelled through narrow spaces. If it is not controlled quickly by trained firefighters, a small fire may suddenly develop into a raging inferno. Wind gusts can shift direction quickly, catching people by surprise as the flames advance faster than people can escape. Rotating winds in a firestorm can also act like a small tornado. These fiery updrafts, called pyronadoes, can reach high into the sky.

Intensity and impacts

Many Australian plants and animals have adapted to life in fire-prone areas. Some plants, such as banksias and native grass trees, need bushfires to break open their seedpods. Other seeds need fire to crack their coats in order to let water in, or they need smoke to help them germinate. But if fires are too intense, too prolonged, too widespread or too regular, many plants and animals simply can't survive – animals may not be able to outrun the flames, or they may not be able to find food or shelter afterwards. Plants that survive or grow back after a big summer of fires may not survive fires the following year. As climate change alters the intensity and length of Australia's fire season, we will all need to be better prepared to manage and control fires.

Fire is waru in the Pitjantjatjara language of the Western Deserts.

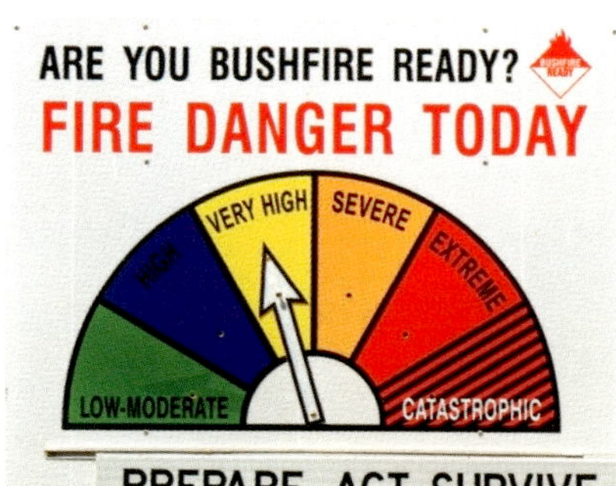

Hakea seedpods require fire to open.

A wallaby returns to a burnt landscape after Australian bushfires.

DID YOU KNOW?

About 70% of plant species in Australia's eucalypt forests can survive bushfires through defence mechanisms that evolved over millions of years.

Spreading smoke

Smoke from bushfires, particularly large ones, can spread many kilometres. In the Black Summer bushfires, smoke spread from Australia all the way around the globe and back again.

It is dangerous to inhale bushfire smoke, so during the 2019–2020 summer, many people in fire-impacted regions were encouraged to stay indoors or to wear masks. Just the smoke from those fires was responsible for the deaths of an estimated 445 people.

Black Summer fires

During the spring and summer of 2019–2020, Australia experienced a catastrophic bushfire season with tragic loss of life and extensive destruction of property, natural landscapes and native and domesticated animals.

A Black Summer bushfire at Mt Solitary in the Blue Mountains, NSW, on the traditional lands of the Gundungurra and Dharug people.

CLIMATE CHANGE

The year 2019 was the hottest and driest year since Australian records began in 1910. It was the second-warmest year globally since 1880. Long-term climate models predict an increase in the duration and intensity of Australia's bushfire season.

AMOUNT OF CARBON DIOXIDE RELEASED:

306 million tonnes

The smoke cloud from the bushfires affected air quality in **New Zealand and South America**

$500 million in bushfire donations

TOTAL AREA BURNT:

17 million+ hectares

more than twice the size of Tasmania

Queensland: **6.6 million ha burnt**
Western Australia: **2 million ha burnt**

IN COMPARISON
2019 Amazon fires: **890,000** hectares burnt
2018 California fires: **809,000** hectares burnt

5900

buildings destroyed

3600

FIREFIGHTERS DEPLOYED INCLUDING:
34 US **66** CANADA **46** NEW ZEALAND

FATALITIES:
AT LEAST

33

including **9** firefighters

AERIAL FIREFIGHTING FLEET:

140 aircraft

including **11** large tankers

55

NSW parks or reserves severely affected by fire (more than 99%)

Darwin
Perth
Adelaide
Melbourne
Hobart

PEOPLE URGED TO EVACUATE:

250,000+

1100

evacuated by ship and **500** by air

$1.34 billion

estimated insurance losses

MORE THAN

3000 homes lost

MORE THAN

1 billion

native animals killed

The 2019–2020 fires were the first to burn such a large amount of area close to human populations, with multiple fires burning simultaneously across the country, many in areas that weren't prone to fire. This resulted in high levels of destruction, including fatalities, houses destroyed and areas burnt, and came at a huge cost to humans and the environment.

Fire danger in Australia is largely monitored by the Forest Fire Danger Index (FFDI), which estimates the potential fire risk based on observations of temperature, rainfall, humidity and wind speed. The Daily FFDI values for spring 2019 were the highest on record for 60% of Australia, significantly higher than the previous highest values in 2002. By the start of September 2019, much of southern Australia was already primed for high fire danger ratings, heralding the start of what would become a catastrophic fire season that would kill at least 33 people, including nine firefighters, destroy more than 3000 homes and burn more than 17 million hectares of land. Nearly 80% of Australians were impacted directly or indirectly by the fires. Of course, this had a devastating impact on native animals and biodiversity, too.

Heatwaves

A heatwave is a period of abnormally hot weather. Heatwaves and bushfires often go hand in hand because high temperatures lead to vegetation (especially grass, twigs, bark and leaves) drying out and becoming flammable. In addition to high temperatures, a bushfire is more likely to occur when the weather is dry (not humid) and windy. In 2019–2020, parts of Australia experienced a record-breaking heatwave that generated extreme fire conditions, contributing to the Black Summer bushfires.

Heatwave impact on vegetation

Plants can only handle so much heat. High temperatures and prolonged exposure to harsh sunlight can stress plants and damage their ability to function. Scientists have found that our native outback plants are being pushed to the limits of survival due to the increasing frequency and intensity of heatwaves.

Crops such as wheat are also negatively affected by heatwaves, because extra heat means less rain is available for crop plants. Heatwaves and drought – a prolonged lack of water – often occur together. Under these sweltering conditions, farmers can't produce as much food.

A drought-affected farm in WA's Wheatbelt.

A HEATWAVE AT BONDI BEACH, NSW

THIRSTY BIRDS
During heatwaves, it is great to put water in birdbaths and troughs to allow birds and other native animals to get a drink and cool down.

Heatwave impact on communities

Even when heatwaves don't cause bushfires, they can be deadly. In fact, heatwaves are responsible for more deaths in Australia than any other natural hazard. In the last 100 years, at least 5000 people have died as a result of heatwaves and heatstroke. At least 420 people perished in the heatwave that happened before the Black Saturday bushfires in 2009.

To stay safe during a heatwave, health professionals recommend staying inside with the blinds closed, the air conditioning on, and with plenty of water and ice to keep you cool and hydrated. This can be difficult – many homes are hard to keep cool, and often people don't have the luxury of air conditioning. Heatwaves have a greater impact on the poor, the elderly and the unwell.

Heatwaves increasing

Australia is set to experience more heatwaves and hot days each year as temperatures increase. Heatwaves are also expected to become more severe. At the same time, days of dangerous fire conditions are increasing, and the fire season is longer, extending into autumn.

Droughts

Droughts result in suffering for people all around Australia, although the biggest impact is on those who live inland. Droughts can cause food crops to fail, farm animals to die, and erosion to increase.

What is drought?

It is difficult to define drought, since it is not simply a matter of low rainfall. If that were the case, most of inland Australia would always be in drought. Scientists monitor a number of factors alongside rainfall, such as soil moisture, ground water levels and social expectations, to decide whether an area is in drought or not. Droughts can last for months, sometimes even years.

Landscape changes

While periods of low rainfall and dryness have occurred regularly in Australia's history, they have been made more intense by the changes to the landscape that occurred after settlement. Extensive land clearing and the introduction of livestock altered the landscape and the climate. When trees are removed, less moisture can evaporate into the atmosphere, leading to more prolonged dry periods and increasing temperatures. When land is cleared, overgrazed or improperly turned over, the top layer of soil may degrade and be swept away by wind.

DRYING OUT

In recent decades, many parts of Australia, including the south-west corner of Western Australia and the eastern coast, have experienced significantly reduced rainfall.

A DRY CREEK BED NEAR WANGARATTA, VIC

DUST STORM IN SYDNEY, NSW

Drought history

Historical reports dating back to the 1860s show that a severe drought has occurred in Australia on average once every 18 years. Two of the most intense were the Federation drought (1895–1903) and the Millennium drought (1997–2009). The Federation drought impacted more than 60 native species across 2.8 million km^2 (more than a third of the nation) and almost halved the number of livestock in the country.

The Millennium drought was the longest uninterrupted period with below-average rainfall in south-eastern Australia since the 1900s. It hugely impacted agriculture in the country and also the supply of clean drinking water. At the beginning of 2017, parts of Australia experienced drought conditions again, although rains in February and March 2021 broke the drought in some areas.

Cracked earth

After no rainfall for years at a time, the soil becomes rocky and hard, and its surface cracks. When rainfall finally arrives after years of desert conditions, the ground may be too hard to absorb the water, which results in sudden flash flooding.

Disappearing streams

Without rain, rivers and lakes can dry up and sometimes disappear completely. Even ground deep below the surface can dry out.

Dust storms

Extreme temperatures cause fast-rising updrafts of air. Strong winds can pick up enormous amounts of dry dirt and dust and carry them many kilometres. The dust from Australian droughts has been found on New Zealand mountaintops and even as far away as Antarctica.

Desertification

Climate change, overgrazing, deforestation and increased soil salinity can all degrade the land, leading to desertification. This is the name for the process of agriculturally productive land turning into desert when nearby sand blows over the land. When agricultural fields are destroyed, farmers have to relocate to find more fertile soil.

Floods

Floods occur when too much rain, brought on by sudden or continuing storms, cannot be absorbed by the soil. Rivers burst their banks, levees are broken and water spills onto the land. Strong ocean winds can also produce huge waves that flood coastal areas. When floodwaters rise slowly, people have time to move to higher ground or build barriers to protect their homes. When water rises too quickly, they can get caught in the flood. Water damages buildings and homes, can wash away vehicles, and even causes some people to drown.

MILTON, QLD, IN FLOOD

Floods in Australia

While Australia is described as the driest inhabited continent on Earth, floods are not uncommon. Dangerous floods have occurred in every Australian state during thunderstorms or periods of heavy rain. While they are damaging for our agriculture and infrastructure, and can be fatal, small inundations are an important part of natural cycles, helping to distribute seeds, animals and sediments to new areas. In northern Australia, it's a seasonal occurrence. During the wet season between November and April, lots of localised storms can cause flooding. First Nations people, who lived in Australia for thousands of years before Europeans arrived, tried to warn settlers not to build towns on the floodplains. Now, town councils and shires have started mapping the historical flood areas for better town planning and building regulations.

Acacia power

Australia has almost a thousand species of acacia (also known as wattle), which are well adapted to coping with cycles of drought and flood. After rains, they produce a lot of flowers. Studying the timing of blooms could help to predict flooding and drought patterns. Acacia trees have very deep roots, which help balance the water levels in soils. In this way, they help to manage floods and release stored water during drought.

Recent floods

Many areas in Australia, particularly in New South Wales and Queensland, were affected by flooding in March 2021. After a summer marked by heavy rainfall brought by La Niña, some areas were inundated to levels not experienced in more than a century. In Sydney, Warragamba Dam was overflowing by about 450 gigalitres a day (nearly as much as all the water in Sydney Harbour), threatening highly populated regions. In New South Wales alone, more than 18,000 people were evacuated.

GOLDEN WATTLE

Namaraag is a word the Dharawal people use for Sydney golden wattle.

MULTIPURPOSE

Species of acacia have long been used by First Nations Australians as food and medicine and also to make tools such as boomerangs, clap sticks and shields.

FLOODS ON YUGGERA COUNTRY IN IPSWICH, QLD

A WURLEY, ILLUSTRATED IN 1886

Flood damage

Floods harm people and habitats in a number of different ways, varying with the type and severity of the flood. The consequences of a flood depend a lot on timing, location, the amount of water and how fast it rises, flows, and dissipates. Since colonisation, many people have died in floods. Surging floodwaters can be deceptively fast or hide dangerous bits of debris – that's why it is so important to never enter floodwaters, either on foot or in a vehicle.

Floods can damage houses, destroy belongings and ruin infrastructure such as roads and bridges. It can take many years for communities to rebuild lost homes and buildings. Farms can also be hard-hit by flooding, with livestock losses, ruined crops and damage to property. Floods move topsoil around, so some farms may lose their fertile soil and suffer a drop in productivity on their land, while other farms may gain new topsoil and have better yields in the years after a flood.

Economic cost

Floods are the most expensive natural disasters in Australia, costing more than $377 million per year. This high cost is due to the large amount of damage floods can cause, coupled with their high frequency compared to other natural disasters.

Indigenous astronomy and meteorology

The Kaurna people of South Australia have traditionally relied on the appearance of a bright star they call Parna to identify when the hot, dry summer is ending and rain, heralding flooding on the Adelaide Plains, is due to arrive. When they spotted the star, they knew it was time to build their waterproof huts, known as wurlies. Other First Nations astronomers can tell just by changes in a star's colour or twinkle that there is more moisture in the air and that floods might be approaching.

Hailstorms

Hail begins as tiny ice pellets. When tiny clumps of ice, kept aloft by strong winds, get blown through freezing thunderclouds, hail is formed. Updraft winds pull the hailstones up, where more droplets attach and freeze as the pellets are thrown up into freezing portions of the cloud. Once the hailstones grow too big to be kept in the air by the updraft, they fall to the ground.

Hailstones

These form in the updrafts inside a type of cloud known as a cumulonimbus. This type of cloud is dense and towering, often seen during storms. The more powerful the updraft in the cloud, the bigger the hailstones.

1 Frozen raindrops made of layers of ice form.

2 Hailstones rise in the updraft and grow larger.

3 Hailstones grow too heavy, and fall to the ground.

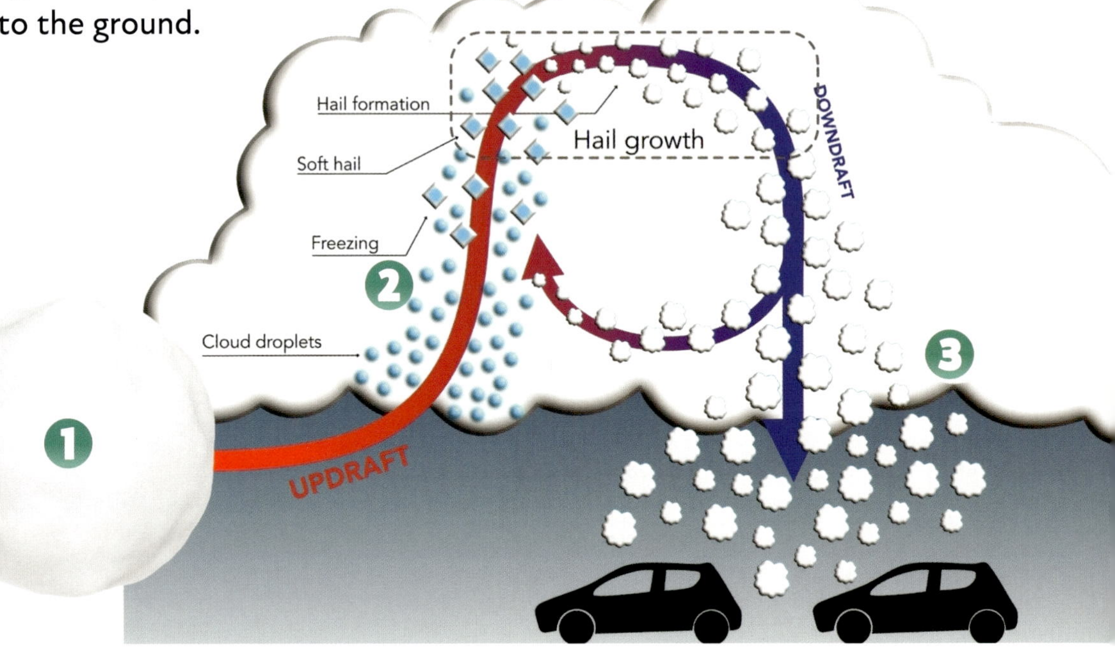

HAIL ON HOMES

Hailstones can cause serious damage. Glass windows may smash, car hoods get dented and roof tiles break.

Our worst hailstorm

On the evening of 14 April 1999, the sky darkened as a thick shelf of cloud began to cast a shadow over Sydney. Residents reported small hail pellets. At this stage, they scarcely suspected that these would turn into ice missiles hurled to the ground at speeds of 200 km/h. But the hail did move in, and calls soon flooded the NSW Fire Brigade. More than 2000 requests for help flooded in over the next five hours, with a call every 10 seconds.

The ice ripped through roofs, dented car bonnets and even damaged aircraft. In the end, 20,000 buildings, 40,000 vehicles and 25 aircraft were affected. The damage bill was $1.7 billion – more than the total cost of 1974's Cyclone Tracy or 1983's Ash Wednesday bushfires. It remains one of the most expensive natural disasters in Australian history (although this is probably due to the cost of Sydney's housing).

Regular damage

It only takes stones 4 cm in diameter, which fall once a year, to break new concrete. Stones 6 cm in diameter fall once every two years, and huge, cricket ball-sized hailstones (8 cm in diameter) hit Sydney every 5–10 years.

The Sydney suburb of Kensington after a hailstorm ripped through in 1999, wrecking thousands of houses, businesses and cars and causing $1.7 billion in damages. Some houses had temporary tarpaulin roofs for months.

Cyclones

Cyclones are large, powerful storms that can reach up to 1000 km across and can generate violent, spiralling winds that exceed 280 km/h. They originate over warm, tropical oceans and generally travel with the direction of the wind, bringing heavy rain and inland flooding when they reach land. Called tropical cyclones in Australia and the Indian Ocean, they are known as hurricanes in the Atlantic, Caribbean and Eastern Pacific, and as typhoons in the Western Pacific.

Bureau of Meteorology tropical storm/cyclone ratings

CATEGORY 5 (280+ km/h)	Trees are uprooted; windows are shattered; small buildings are overturned; structural damage occurs to large buildings.
CATEGORY 4 (225–279 km/h)	Some road signs are blown down; major damage occurs to buildings (especially to roofs, windows and doors).
CATEGORY 3 (165–224 km/h)	Large trees are blown down; small buildings suffer structural damage; mobile homes are destroyed.
CATEGORY 2 (125–164 km/h)	Trees are blown down; major damage occurs to doors, windows and roofing materials.
CATEGORY 1 (Up to 125 km/h)	Wind can cause damage to shrubs and mobile homes.

FACT

Northern Australia often experiences cyclones, which are known as burrmalala in the Yolŋu Matha language of Arnhem Land, NT.

Cyclone formation

The warm ocean heats the air above, increasing the level of water vapour in the air. When the moisture condenses into clouds, the air pressure drops and strong winds are created. These strong winds spin faster as they move across the ocean, and a cyclone is born.

Inside a cyclone

1. A mature cyclone consists of bands of thunderclouds.
2. The eye is a clear, almost calm area at the centre of the storm.
3. Bands are fed by warm, moist updrafts as they spiral towards the eye.
4. The air is warmest and circulates fastest at the base.
5. In the upper levels, the air spirals outward from the cyclone's centre.
6. As the cyclone approaches land, a storm surge can drive seawater deep inland.

Cyclone destruction

Cyclones are a fact of life for northern Australians, who face alerts and storms each wet season from November to April. Despite improved warning systems and coordinated responses, the biggest cyclones always wreak havoc.

CYCLONE TRACY – CAT. 4

Cyclone Tracy struck Darwin on Christmas morning 1974, with winds of more than 200 km/h, leaving more than half the city's 43,000 inhabitants homeless. Within weeks, three-quarters of the population had chosen to leave or were evacuated. Many never returned. Seventy-one people died and 80% of the city was devastated.

CYCLONE MARCIA – CAT. 5

Cyclone Marcia intensified to category 5 just before crossing the Queensland coast in February 2015. With wind gusts of almost 300 km/h, it destroyed about 350 homes and damaged 2000 properties around Yeppoon and Rockhampton.

CYCLONE SEROJA – CAT. 3

Having already caused flooding, landslides and more than 100 deaths in Indonesia and Timor-Leste, Cyclone Seroja hit WA between Geraldton and Kalbarri in April 2021 with wind gusts of up to 170 km/h. It destroyed homes and caused long power outages.

CYCLONE DAMAGE, QLD

Tornadoes

Tornadoes are powerful, twisting funnels of rising wind that reach down from supercell thunderstorms and hit the ground. Some tornadoes last just a few seconds, while others may go on for more than an hour.

A tornado forms when warmer moist air mixes with colder dry air inside the thunderstorm. A change of wind direction makes a column of air rotate and spiral towards the ground. Australia rarely experiences this type of natural disaster, but some tornadoes have occurred.

FIRE TORNADO

Tornado or cyclone?

A tornado is a narrow, rotating column of air that lasts for a short time. Cyclones are large storms that can be hundreds of kilometres wide and last for days.

Tornado formation

When warm, moist air meets cool, dry air, instability is created in the atmosphere. A change in wind direction and an increase in wind speed can create a horizontal spinning tube of air in the lower atmosphere. The rising air of a thundercloud tilts the tube of air from the horizontal to vertical, and a funnel cloud forms.

Funnel clouds are rotating cone-shaped columns of air that extend downward from the base of a thunderstorm, but they do not touch the ground. If they do, a tornado is formed. Most tornadoes begin as funnel clouds, but not all funnel clouds become tornadoes. A tornado funnel can range from 3 m across to wider than 1.6 km.

Destruction

Extensive damage occurs when a tornado touches down. Changes in wind speed and direction send the main funnel on a path of destruction. Most tornadoes rarely last longer than 10 minutes, but even in a small amount of time, they can cause lots of damage, uplifting cars and ripping roofs off buildings. Usually occurring in spring, when the weather is warmer, tornadoes kill hundreds of people across the world each year.

Fire tornadoes

During intense bushfires, such as those of the 2019–2020 Black Summer, fire tornadoes can occur. They come in different sizes and intensities and are formed in different ways depending on environmental conditions. They most commonly occur when hot, strong winds come into contact with already raging bushfires. Updraughts of hot air catch the fire, and surrounding winds send it whirling into the air, sucking up debris and flammable gases.

KIRRIBILLI, NSW

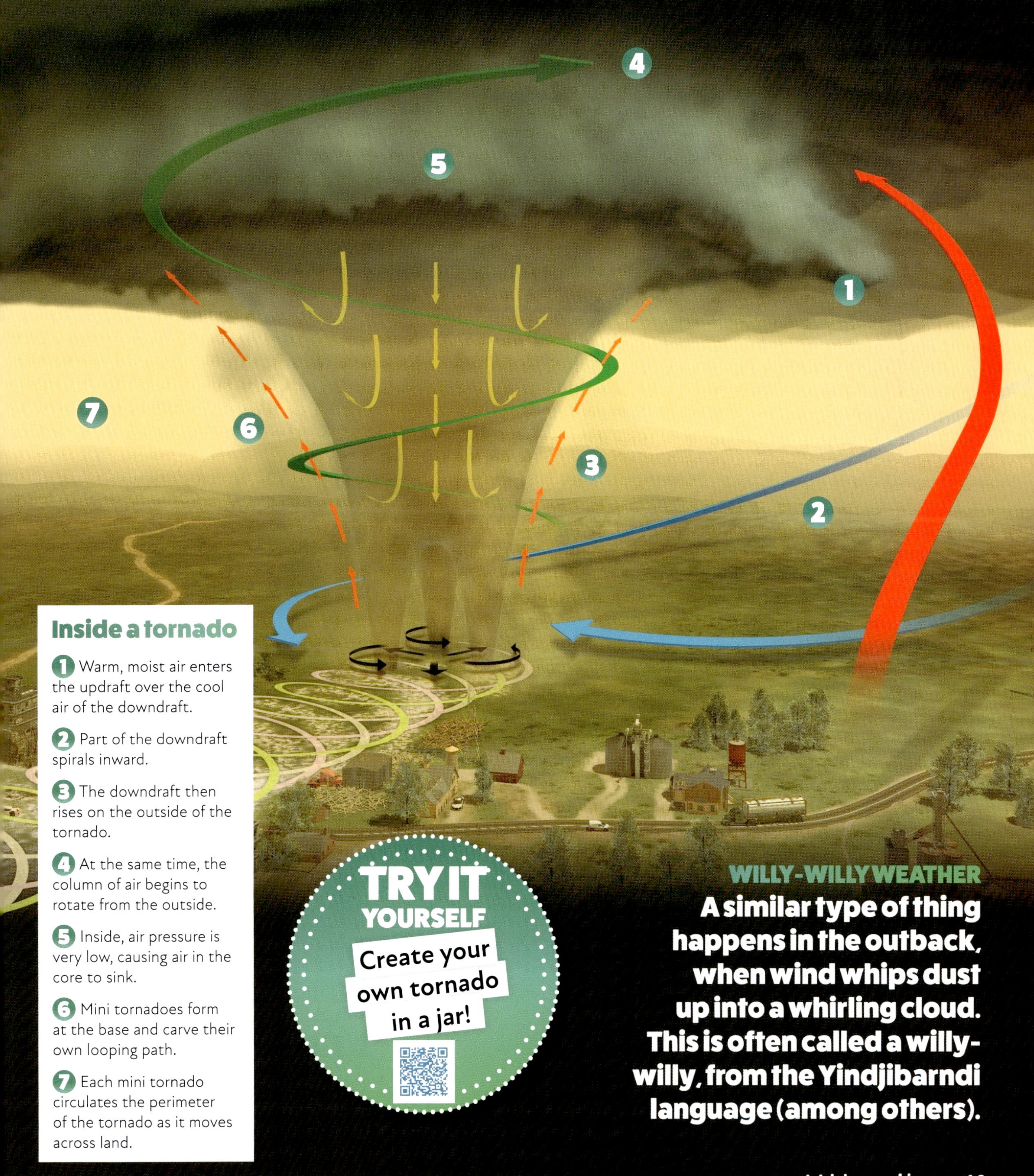

Inside a tornado

1. Warm, moist air enters the updraft over the cool air of the downdraft.
2. Part of the downdraft spirals inward.
3. The downdraft then rises on the outside of the tornado.
4. At the same time, the column of air begins to rotate from the outside.
5. Inside, air pressure is very low, causing air in the core to sink.
6. Mini tornadoes form at the base and carve their own looping path.
7. Each mini tornado circulates the perimeter of the tornado as it moves across land.

WILLY-WILLY WEATHER

A similar type of thing happens in the outback, when wind whips dust up into a whirling cloud. This is often called a willy-willy, from the Yindjibarndi language (among others).

Plate tectonics

Our planet is not simply a solid ball of rock. Of Earth's layers, only the inner and innermost cores are solid. The outer core is so hot that it is liquid. The mantle is mostly solid rock mixed with rocks that have melted to form a thick liquid called magma. The Earth's crust is made of vast, rocky slabs, called tectonic plates, of around 100 km thick. They 'float' on the lower part of the mantle – a layer of molten rock known as the asthenosphere – and move constantly.

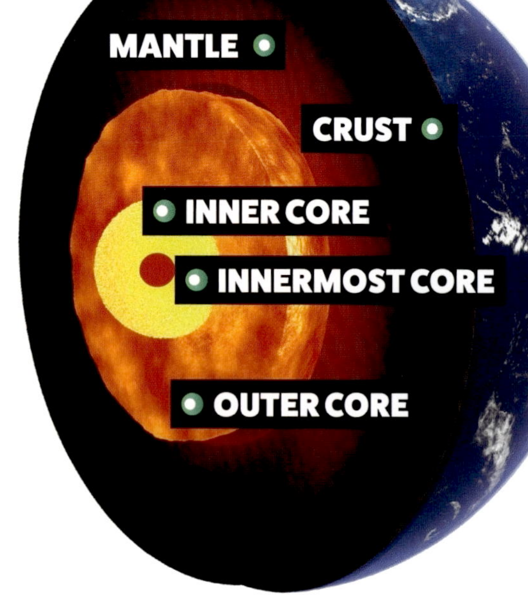

When plates collide

When the plates hit each other, they can cause earthquakes, or they may be pushed up to form mountains. If magma from the mantle comes up through these mountains, they can erupt as volcanoes. Seven of these plates are very large and roughly correspond to the Earth's continents – the African, Antarctic, Eurasian, North American, South American, Pacific and Indo-Australian plates. Most earthquakes and volcanoes occur at the boundaries of these plates.

1. When thin plates under the ocean collide, hot magma can force its way up to form island volcanoes.

2. When these collide, they can produce high mountain ranges. The Eurasian and Indian plates collided many years ago to form the Himalayas in Asia.

3. As the plates move, they grind, push and stick against each other, and huge forces can build up. If the plates move suddenly, the violent vibration is felt as an earthquake.

4. Near the coast, where the crust is still thin, magma can force its way upward to form volcanoes.

5. Under the ocean, one tectonic plate may move under another. Where this occurs, the ocean floor is much deeper than usual.

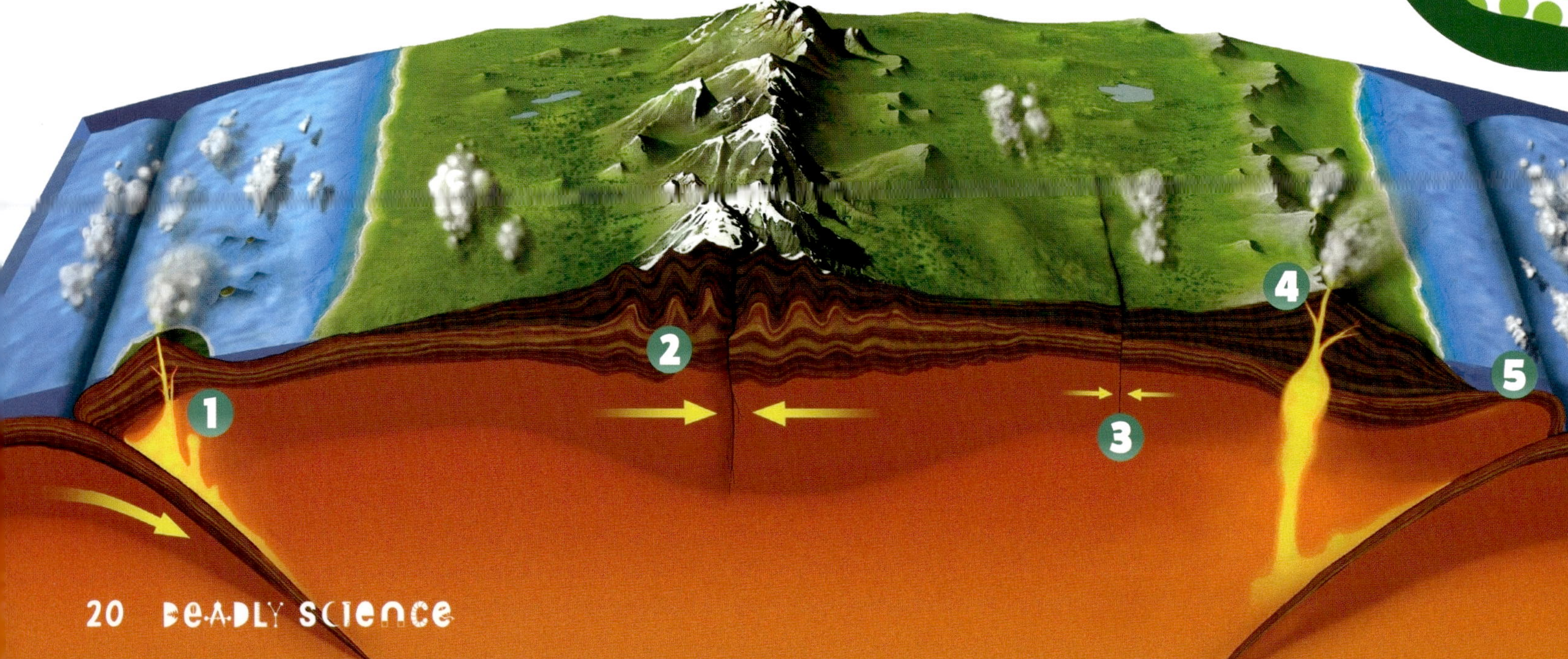

TECTONIC PLATES

Of the 15-20 known tectonic plates, some are continental (under landmasses) and some are oceanic (under bodies of water).

DID YOU KNOW?

In 2023, seismologists at Australian National University measured reverberations from earthquakes to find that the Earth has another layer! Called the innermost core, this 650-km wide solid ball has a slightly different structure to the inner core.

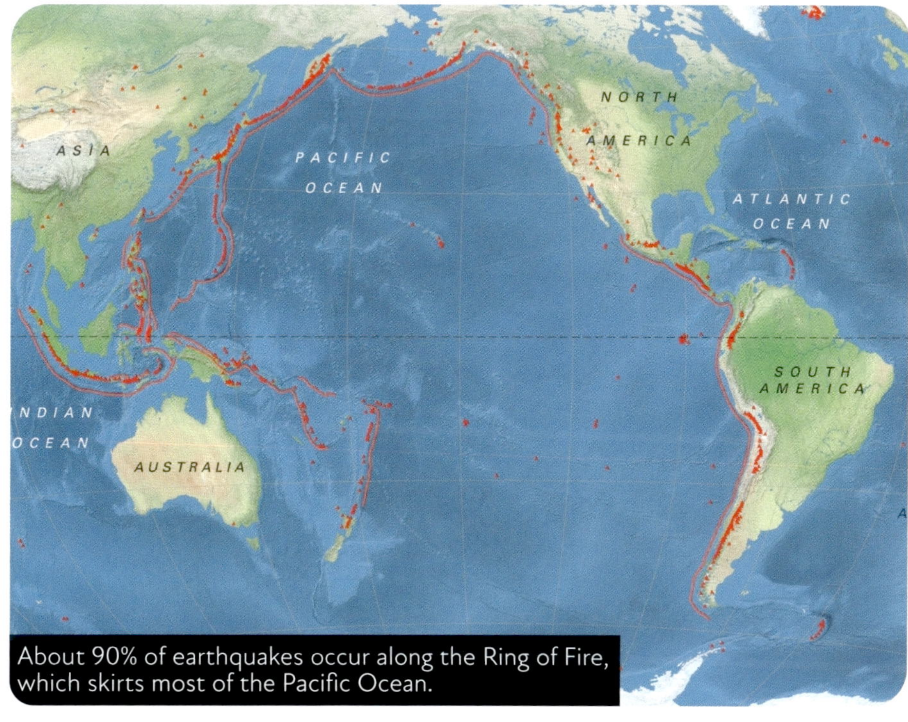

About 90% of earthquakes occur along the Ring of Fire, which skirts most of the Pacific Ocean.

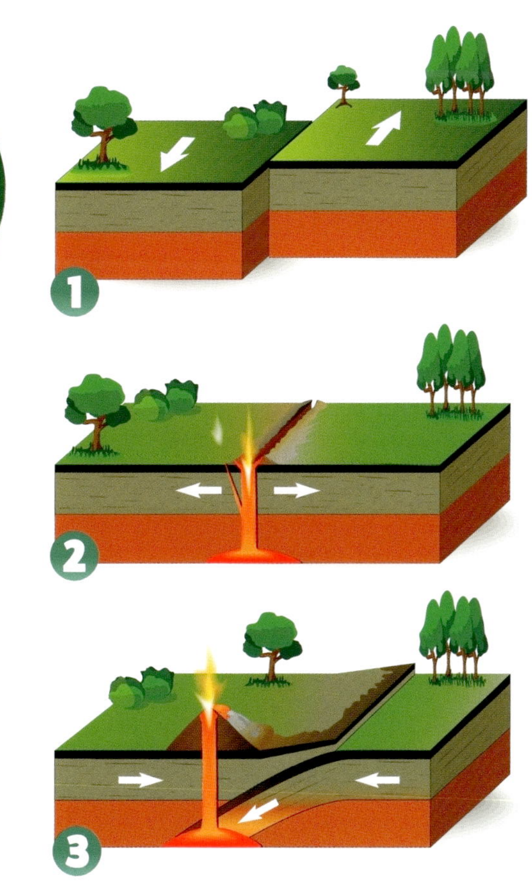

Plate boundaries

The part of the Earth's crust where two plates meet is called a plate boundary. Movement in the hot mantle causes the plates to move in different directions.

1 Two plates that slide in opposite directions past each other create a transform fault or boundary.

2 A divergent boundary, where two plates move away from each other, thins or creates a gap in the Earth's crust.

3 A convergent boundary is one where two plates move towards or collide with each other.

Ring of Fire

The Ring of Fire is the belt of weakness in the Earth's crust that extends 40,000 km from South America to the Alaskan peninsula, across to Japan, the Philippines, Indonesia, and on through the Melanesian islands to New Zealand. The Ring is made up of mountain ranges, ocean trenches and 452 volcanoes, and is characterised by high levels of seismic activity – which means earthquakes. The Ring traces around the Pacific Plate, which is the tectonic plate below the Pacific Ocean. Dramatic geological events occur when this plate bumps against the plates that surround it.

Earthquakes

As the two sides of fractured rock at a fault line strain against each other, stress builds up. When one side or the other eventually gives way, there is a jolt. Vibrations pass through the rock as the built-up stress or energy is released as an earthquake. Every year, half a million earthquakes occur worldwide. Only about 100,000 of these are strong enough to be felt, and only about 100 are big enough to cause damage. Shallow earthquakes tend to cause the most damage.

Earthquakes in Australia

Because Australia sits in the middle of a tectonic plate, earthquakes here aren't very common. The Australian plate is the fastest-moving continental landmass on Earth and is pushing against plates to the north and east approximately 7 cm a year. When this stress builds up, rocks break and slide along fault lines. In Australia, an average of 100 earthquakes of magnitude 3 or more are recorded each year. An earthquake above magnitude 5 occurs every 1–2 years.

Damage

When a major earthquake occurs, some damage is obvious. Buildings may collapse, bridges fall and chasms open. It's often the less-obvious damage, however, that causes problems in the days and weeks to come. Live powerlines can be knocked down and may electrocute anyone who comes in contact with them. When power is cut, often to large areas, normal life becomes difficult. Split or cracked roads make it hard to get emergency supplies into affected areas. Broken water pipes may leak much-needed fresh water. Leaking gas pipes can be lethal. Smashed drainage pipes can cause disease. And the aftershocks that commonly follow an earthquake may cause damaged buildings to collapse, up to weeks or even years later.

Predicting quakes

There is still no method to predict the exact time, place or magnitude of an earthquake. Seismologists, who study the internal structure of the Earth, use the location of faults to predict the general area in which major earthquakes are most likely to occur.

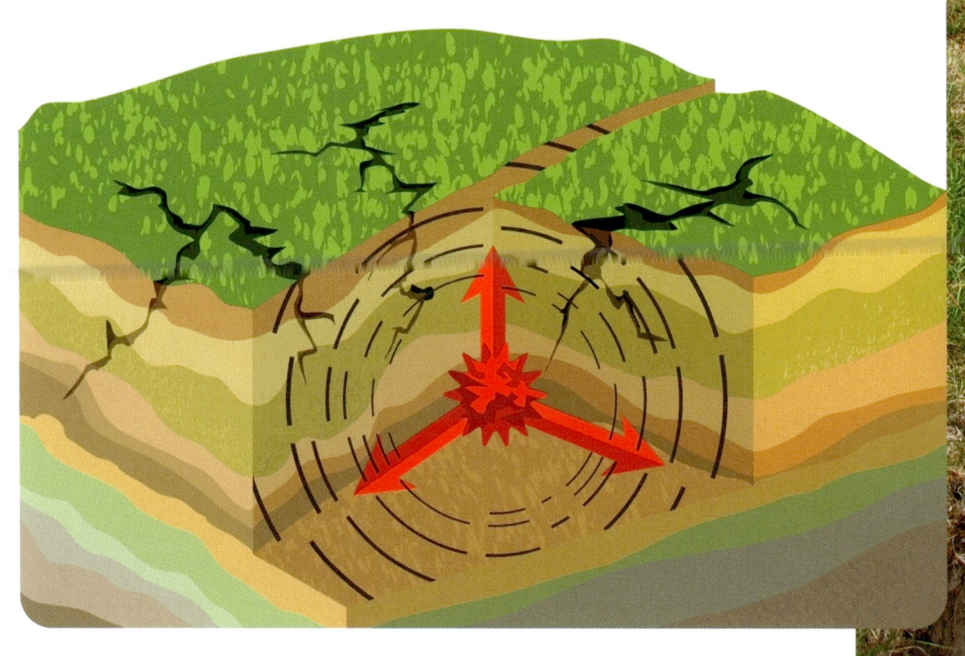

CHRISTCHURCH, NZ

NEWCASTLE WORKERS CLUB, NSW

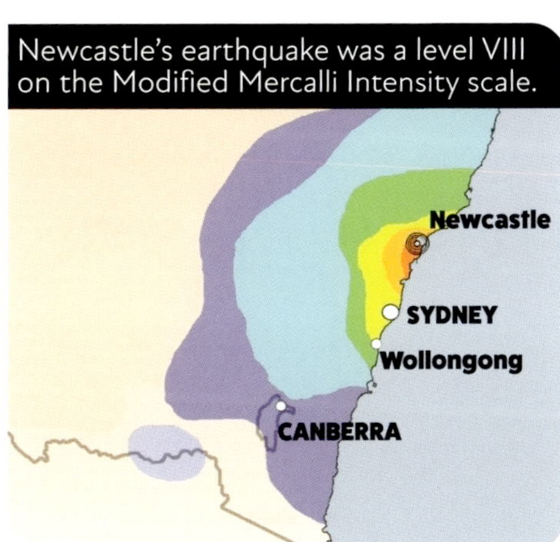
Newcastle's earthquake was a level VIII on the Modified Mercalli Intensity scale.

CLOSE TO HOME

The 2011 earthquake in Christchurch, New Zealand, killed 185 people and wrecked the city's CBD.

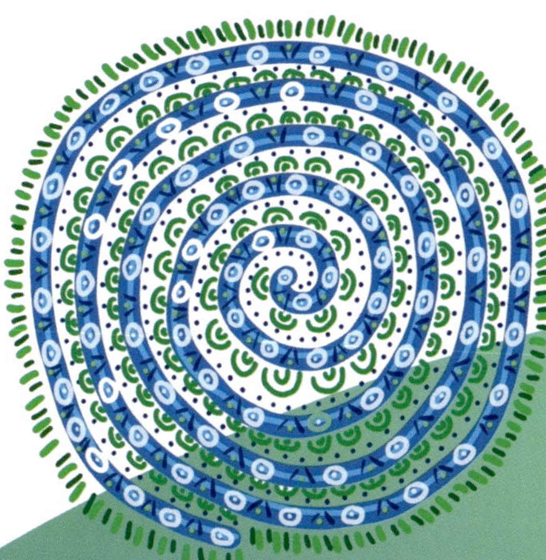

Newcastle quake

On 28 December 1989, the city of Newcastle, NSW, was devastated, as one of the most disastrous earthquakes in Australian history struck. People were seen leaving their offices and spilling onto the streets while buildings crumbled around them. Thirteen people died, and many of the city's historical buildings were decimated, along with approximately 35,000 homes, resulting in about 1000 displaced people and a $4 billion damage bill. In total, about 50,000 buildings were damaged, and roughly 300 had to be demolished. This destruction and distress resulted in one of Australia's worst natural disasters, despite the earthquake only registering magnitude 5.6 on the Richter scale.

It struck about 15 km south-west of Newcastle's CBD at an estimated (and relatively shallow) depth of 11 km. The quake was amplified by soft sediments deposited from the Hunter River, which intensified ground motion and caused more severe building damage.

Measuring earthquakes

Two measures of earthquake intensity, or magnitude, are commonly used today. The Modified Mercalli Intensity scale measures the effects of an earthquake on the environment, as reported by observers. No instruments are required, as the scale relies on eyewitness reports. The Richter scale uses a seismograph to measure earthquake intensity.

SEISMOGRAPH

KAIKOURA, NZ

Richter scale

The Richter scale measures the size, or amplitude, of the largest horizontal seismic motion recorded. For each number on the Richter scale, the recorded amplitude goes up by a factor of 10. A magnitude 2 earthquake therefore has 10 times the amplitude of a magnitude 1 earthquake.

Earthquake intensity

	MAGNITUDE	
	1–2	Detected only by seismographs near the epicentre.
	2–3	Might be felt by some people near the epicentre.
	3–4	People feel slight tremors; lights swing; there is little damage.
	4–5	Strong tremors are felt; windows crack; buildings are damaged.
	5–6	Very strong tremors are felt; people start to panic; walls crack.
	7–8	This is a severe earthquake; chimneys fall; some buildings collapse.
	8–9	The ground cracks; more buildings collapse; widespread panic.
	10	Massive destruction; bridges collapse; train tracks and roads buckle.

Modified Mercalli Intensity (MMI) Scale

Giuseppe Mercalli's 1902 seismic intensity scale had 10 (X) degrees. Two more degrees were later added, describing the effects of an earthquake on natural features, industrial installations and human beings. This modified scale is used today.

I	**Not felt**	Not felt, except by a very few.
II	**Weak**	Felt by only a few people at rest, especially on the upper floors of tall buildings.
III	**Weak**	Noticeable by people indoors, especially on upper floors of buildings. Standing cars may rock slightly. Vibrations similar to the passing of a truck.
IV	**Light**	Felt indoors by many, outdoors by few during the day. At night, some are awakened. Dishes, windows, doors rattled; walls made cracking sounds. Sensations like heavy trucks striking buildings. Standing cars rocked noticeably.
V	**Moderate**	Felt by nearly everyone; many awakened. Some dishes, windows broken. Unstable objects overturned. Pendulum clocks may stop.
VI	**Strong**	Felt by all, many frightened. Some heavy furniture moved; a few instances of fallen plaster. Damage slight.
VII	**Very strong**	Frightens all persons; some can't stand. Damage negligible in buildings of good design and construction; slight-to-moderate damage in well-built structures; considerable damage in poorly built or badly designed structures.
VIII	**Severe**	Damage slight in specially designed structures; considerable damage in ordinary substantial buildings with partial collapse. Damage great in poorly built structures. Fall of chimneys, factory stacks, columns, monuments, walls. Heavy furniture overturned.
IX	**Violent**	Damage considerable in specially designed structures. Damage great in substantial buildings, with partial collapse. Buildings shifted off foundations. Landslides.
X	**Extreme**	Some well-built wooden structures destroyed; most masonry, frame and foundations of structures destroyed. Rails bent. Open cracks and broad wavy folds in roads.
XI	**Extreme**	Most well-built wooden and masonry structures destroyed; bridges destroyed. Rails bent greatly. Specially designed earthquake-resistant buildings may have minor damage. Underground pipelines out of service. Landslides.
XII	**Extreme**	Almost total devastation of all poor-to-moderately built structures. Specially designed structures damages. Waves seen on ground surfaces. Landslides.

SEVERE QUAKE

An earthquake in Ecuador had a Modified Mercalli Intensity score of VIII (severe); more than 700 people died.

PORTOVIEJO, ECUADOR

Tsunamis

Tsunamis can be generated by any significant displacement of water in oceans or lakes, although they are most commonly created by the movement of tectonic plates under the ocean floor during an earthquake. They can also be caused by volcanic eruptions, glacial carving, meteorite impacts or landslides. As each tsunami is unique, and not all earthquakes produce them, there is still little known about where the worst waves will strike and how big they will be.

Tsunami formation

An earthquake under the ocean jolts the seabed upward. An enormous amount of water is displaced and begins to move outward from the epicentre. Tsunamis begin with a deep-sea movement of water and can travel at a staggering 1000 km/h. In shallower water, the tsunami slows down, but the column of water behind it moves slightly faster, and as it catches up, it piles on top and the wave grows in height. Often, a tsunami isn't a single wave but a series of waves separated by between 5–90 minutes.

Tsunamis long ago

There is evidence that monumental tsunamis have pummelled the east coast of Australia throughout history – and could do so again. Based on sediment layers and rock erosion, scientists believe six big tsunamis, which were caused by meteorite strikes or marine landslides, have hit the Sydney region during the past 10,000 years. The most recent big one probably occurred in 1491, and produced a wave that washed over the harbour's headlands, 60 m above sea level. That particular tsunami didn't travel far inshore, but others did.

There is evidence a tsunami hit the Shoalhaven delta on the NSW south coast between 4000 and 5000 years ago and ran 10 km inland. Deposits near the Blue Mountains hint that another tsunami ran over cliffs more than 60 m high and then rushed inland. A similar event today would have the potential for widespread destruction.

First Nations stories reveal evidence of tsunamis and other instances of extreme weather. A story from the Burragorang people tells of a time when stars fell from the sky (not unlike meteors) and led to a period of great rain and water covering the whole land from horizon to horizon.

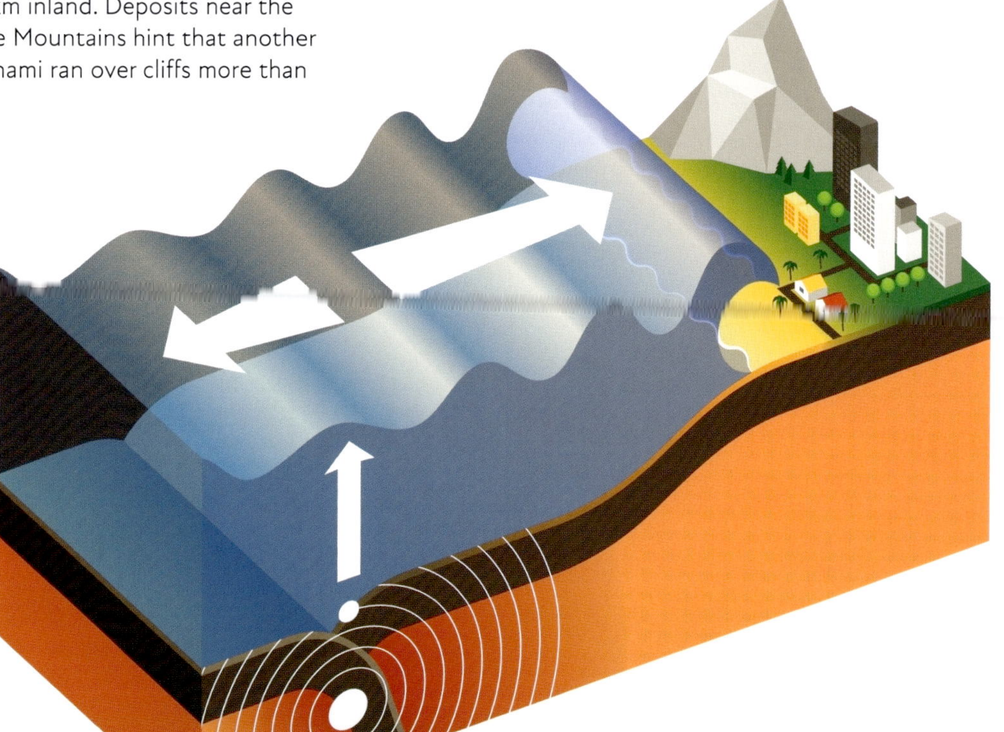

2004 BOXING DAY TSUNAMI

The devastating Indian Ocean tsunami was caused by an earthquake with an MMI scale of up to IX (violent) in some locations. The earthquake happened along the boundary between the Burma and Indian plates.

Recent tsunamis

About 50 tsunamis have hit Australia since 1805. The biggest was triggered by a quake just off Java in 2006. The resulting tsunami hit north-western Australia with a height of 10 m, flooding 500 m inland. The area is sparsely populated, so no one in Australia was killed; but 600 people died in Java.

The largest in the world was the Alaska tsunami of 1958, at 524 m high, but the most devastating was the Boxing Day tsunami of 2004, which struck Indonesia, Sri Lanka, the Maldives, India and Thailand. More than 227,000 people died.

TRY IT YOURSELF

See how a tsunami impacts a coastline!

The aftermath in Banda Aceh, Indonesia, after the 2004 Indian Ocean tsunami destroyed it.

Volcanoes

Magma is very hot, thick liquid rock. It forms when great heat causes rock in the Earth's mantle to melt. This melted rock then forms into large underground chambers. In some places, magma is forced up through the Earth's crust. The places where this happens are called hot spots. As a tectonic plate moves very slowly over a hot spot, a volcano can form above it.

Oceanic hot spot

When hot spots occur below the ocean, volcanoes grow up slowly from the sea floor. At first, erupting magma forms an underwater volcano, which grows until it emerges above the ocean surface as a volcanic island. It takes these volcanoes about a million years to reach the ocean surface. As tectonic plates shift, this can slowly form whole island chains, such as Hawaii.

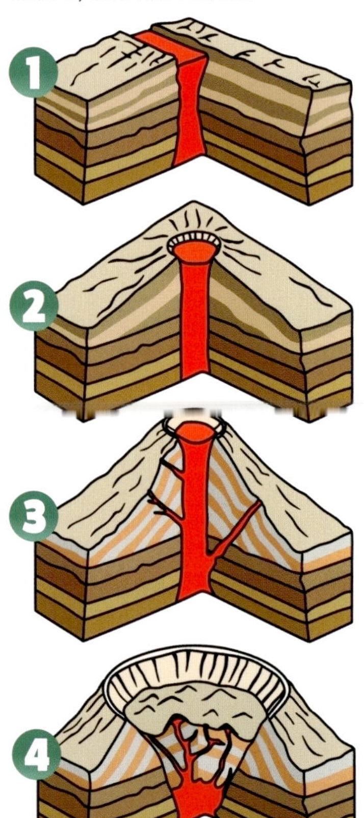

Channels and vents

The inside of a volcano is made up of solid rock. Within this rock are chambers or channels of hot magma. At times, magma forces its way through a side channel and comes out through a vent in the side of the volcano.

Volcano types

There are different kinds of volcanoes. They are formed from different types of rock, have different shapes to each other and erupt in different ways.

1. **FISSURE** These volcanoes form when magma erupts through a crack in the Earth's surface.
2. **SHIELD** Broad, low volcanoes formed from low-viscosity runny lava that spreads more widely.
3. **STRATOVOLCANO** When these erupt, they build up layers of ash and lava. They are cone shaped and steep sided.
4. **CINDER CONE** Eruptions build up cone-shaped hills of cinders with wide craters.

Parts of a volcano

1. **CRATER** Located inside the top of the volcano, the crater is usually the major source of lava and gases in an eruption.
2. **DYKE** When magma cuts up through the layers of surrounding rock, it is called a dyke and may emerge through the surface as a vent.
3. **CENTRAL CONDUIT** The channel that leads from the chamber of magma to the crater.
4. **CONE** The outside of the volcano. It is built up from lava and ash from earlier eruptions.
5. **SIDE VENT** Magma flows out through a vent in the side of the volcano. Once erupted, magma is called lava. Each layer of lava makes the volcano higher and wider.
6. **LACCOLITH** Some magma flows into a chamber called a laccolith. It cools down and does not flow to the surface.
7. **MAGMA** Hot, melted rock.
8. **ASH** A mixture of rock, mineral and glass particles that come out during an eruption.

MT ELEPHANT, VIC

ANCIENT CRATERS

In the Dreaming, Mt Elephant (Djerrinallum in Wathawurrung language) was created when two spirits fought over a stone axe and were both mortally wounded.

UNDARA LAVA TUNNEL, QLD

Volcanoes in Australia

There are no active volcanoes on the Australian mainland, but First Nations peoples living thousands of years ago witnessed eruptions. The most recent of these were between 4500–5000 years ago at Mt Schank and Mt Gambier in South Australia, and there is still evidence of Australia's volcanic activity – from remnant volcanoes found in Victoria to the lava fields of Undara in Queensland.

However, active volcanoes are present on the Australian external territory of Heard Island and McDonald Islands, as well as in many of our neighbouring nations, including New Zealand, Indonesia and Papua New Guinea.

The impacts of large eruptions can be felt a great distance away. When Mt Krakatoa in Indonesia erupted in 1883, the force was four times greater than any bomb ever detonated, and the noise was heard as far away as Perth.

Volcano case study: Jilkminggan School

Deadly Scientists in the Jalmurrak class at Jilkminggan School in the Northern Territory were learning about natural disasters. Students learnt how volcanoes are formed and what happens when they erupt. During Science Week, they made their own exploding volcanoes.

Students investigated the different forms magma and lava can take and worked to label the different parts of a volcano. They experimented with the consistency of dough to build their volcanoes and the combination of different materials that can create a volcanic eruption. Students observed that a combination of baking soda and vinegar created the eruption with the most pressure. DeadlyScience donated science experiment books that have inspired these young scientists.
– Tameka Lewis,
Jilkminggan School, NT

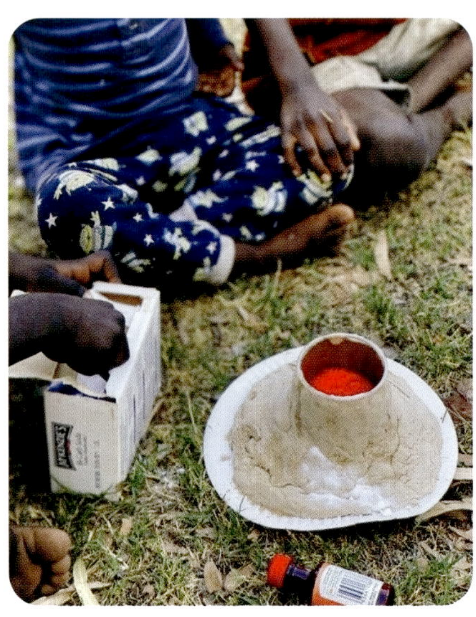

SHAWNEE BAKER

TRY IT YOURSELF

Make your own exploding volcano by following these steps!

Materials

- 2 small plastic bottles
- Large baking tray
- Building material – dough/soil/plasticine/papier mache
- 1 tbsp bicarbonate of soda
- 2 tbsp water
- 1 tbsp dishwashing liquid
- Red food colouring
- ½ cup vinegar

Steps

1. Go outside, or put down some sheets to catch the eruption. Set an empty bottle upright in the middle of the baking tray and remove the cap.
2. Shape your building material firmly around the bottle to make a volcano, and then decorate it. Don't cover the top of the bottle.
3. Put the bicarbonate of soda in the other bottle and add water.
4. Add the dishwashing liquid and a few drops of red food colouring and mix well. Carefully pour the mixture into your volcano's bottle core.
5. When you are ready, pour the vinegar into the core – and watch your volcano erupt!

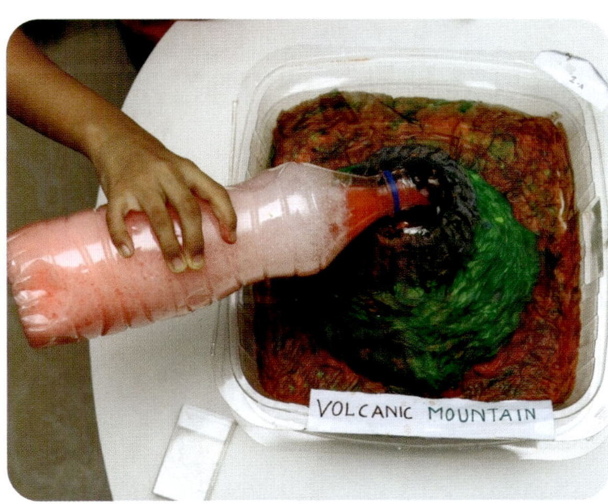

CHEMICAL REACTION

When you mix bicarbonate of soda and vinegar, they react to make a gas called carbon dioxide. The gas builds up inside the bottle until it erupts. Beneath the Earth's crust, magma does the same thing. It rises up through cracks in the rocks and bursts out as lava.

Hardie Grant acknowledges the Traditional Owners of the Country on which we work, the Wurundjeri People of the Kulin Nation and the Gadigal People of the Eora Nation, and recognises their continuing connection to the land, waters and culture. We pay our respects to their Elders past and present.

Hardie Grant Children's Publishing
Wurundjeri Country
Level 11, 36 Wellington Street
Collingwood Victoria 3066
Melbourne | Sydney | San Francisco
hardiegrant.com/childrens
www.australiangeographic.com.au
ISBN: 9781761216664
First published 2022
This edition published 2025

Series editor Corey Tutt **Illustrator** Mim Cole / Mimmim
Designer Hannah Chapman

Publisher Penelope White **Editorial** Savannah Hollis with Olivia Brown
Cover design Andy Warren **Internal design** Hannah Janzen
Production Sally Davis

Printed in China by LEO Paper Products LTD

The paper this book is printed on is from FSC® certified forests and other controlled sources. FSC® promotes environmentally responsible, socially beneficial and economically viable management of the world's forests.

10 9 8 7 6 5 4 3 2 1

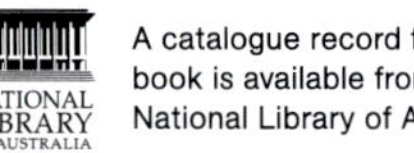

A catalogue record for this book is available from the National Library of Australia

Picture credits

Front Cover: adike/Shutterstock (SS); Roman Mikhailiuk/SS; Anne Hayes/Australian Geographic (AG); Siberian Art/SS; ONYXprj/SS; Rosliak Nataliia/SS; Nataliia/AdobeStock. **3:** Don Fuchs/AG; Designua/SS; **4:** Quentin Chester/AG; myphotobank.com.au/SS; **5:** Karl Hofman/SS; Quentin Chester/AG; Daria Nipot/SS; **6:** Leah-Anne Thompson/SS; **7:** Will Pringle and Mike Rossi/AG; **8:** idiz/SS; Marianne Purdy/SS; Peter B Ryan/SS; **9:** Big Dane/SS; Big Dane/SS; **10:** Campbell Mattinson/SS; **11:** G Tipene/SS; Thomas Wielecki/AG; **12:** Brisbane/SS; StevanZZ/SS; **13:** wallaby/SS; A. Irwin/Picturesque Atlas of Australia/NLA; **14:** ILYA AKINSHIN/Adobestock; Jamestorm/SS; Andreanicolini /SS. **15:** John Carnemolla/SS; **16:** Jacques Descloitres/MODIS Rapid Response Team/NASA/GSFC; **17:** Australian Geographic; Inge Blessas/SS. **18:** Adansijav Official/SS; PominOz/Dreamstime; **19:** Australian Geographic. **20:** Diego Barucco/SS; Australian Geographic. **21:** Will Pringle/AG; Designua/SS; **22:** Lakeview Images/SS; mapichai/SS; **23:** Newcastle City Library; Bidgee/Geoscience Australia/Wikimedia Commons; **24:** Igor Tichonow/SS; one step aside/SS; gritsalak karalak/SS; **25:** Fotos593/SS; **26:** VectorMine/SS; **27:** Frans Delian/SS; **28:** VectorMine/SS; udaix/SS; **29:** Don Fuchs/AG; Drew Hopper/AG; **30:** All Tameka Lewis/Jilkminggan School; **31:** All Santhosh Varghese/SS.